A Miracle in the Middle of a Valley

S A M U E L R I C H A R D S O N

authorHOUSE®

AuthorHouse™
1663 Liberty Drive
Bloomington, IN 47403
www.authorhouse.com
Phone: 1 (800) 839-8640

Published by AuthorHouse 04/27/2017

ISBN: 978-1-5246-2737-9 (sc)
ISBN: 978-1-5246-2736-2 (e)

Library of Congress Control Number: 2016914359

Print information available on the last page.

Contents

Acknowledgments

Samuel Richardson & Margret Whitaker

I am thankful for my mother, Margret Whitaker, who took the time to stop by the Ocala, Florida, orphanage where I was at the age of five, sitting on the porch with my younger brother and sister. She made the decision to take me into her home, and she raised me as her own. Her sister took my brother, and a Caucasian family took my sister; I never saw her again. I often wonder what happened to my sister and if she had a good life.

It was the worst time in my life, not knowing how I would find food for me and my siblings when I did not know how to take care of myself. I often wondered what I did that was so terrible that no one wanted me or loved me. It was a very scary and lonely time; no words can express how I felt. Living in an orphanage was not an ideal situation, but it was so much better than being homeless at the age of five, with my younger brother and sister. I endured things that no child or adult should have to endure. If she did not take me into her home, I may not be alive today. Because of my mother's caring heart, I am the man I am today.

Special thanks also to Brother Bruce Bolden, who has been by my side for many years. He is the deacon at my church and remains very humble and ready to serve at a moment's notice. He has been there for me when others have gone in a different direction. Not once has he ever complained all these years. He is a trustworthy, dependable, and spiritually minded individual. He is not above doing whatever needs to be done to help the church grow, including cutting the grass, painting, and cleaning. No task is too small for him to take on.

Introduction

I am Pastor Samuel Richardson, born May 9, 1927, in Ocala, Florida. I had one brother, Elijah Richardson, and a sister, Rosetta Richardson. I am just a meager servant of God who is not worthy of the gift that God has given me. I am not an educated man, and I never knew my parents; sometimes, I feel all alone in this world. Now, at the age of ninety, I still regret not getting educated and not having family as others do. I often wonder where my uncle, cousins, nieces, and nephews are and why I do not have family to attend reunions with, and it sometimes makes me feel empty and very sad.

I sometimes wonder why I was given the gift of prophecy and healing when I sometimes feel unequipped to minister His precious gift. I feel that if I were more educated, people would accept what I have to say. There have been times when I did not tell people what God told me to tell them because I felt inadequate and could not approach those people due to their status. Later, I realized that I could have saved them from pain and hurt if I had been confident enough to approach them. I know this is a way that Satan tries to push me off track, but through fasting and praying, I press on. I've realized that God gives His gift to whomever He desires, and it requires no special skills to receive His precious mercy, love, and gifts. I wrote this book in hopes that it encourages others to press forward and do God's will no matter how inadequate they might feel. "I have planted, Apollos watered; but God gave the increase" (1 Corinthians 3:6).

The valley is a low place between hills and mountains with water flowing through it. Even though the valley is a low place, it still produces everything that the animals traveling through it need to survive, just as the spirit of God produces for us when we are in a low place in life. We must travel the low places in order to know how to navigate the high places in life; without a foundation, we have nothing to build on. "Nevertheless the foundation of God standeth sure, having this seal, The Lord knoweth them that are his. And, let everyone that nameth the name of Christ depart from iniquity" (2 Timothy 2:19).

God brought me through the valley with no education when I was five and my brother, my sister, and I were foster children, left on the front porch of a closed foster-care facility. And God still holds my hand and teaches me, Samuel Richardson Sr., at the age of ninety how to teach others His will. I am very careful to not mislead anyone but to help and encourage each individual with all that God has given me.

Chapter 1

The Beginning

God is still leading me because I still have no education, but I adhere to the spirit of God to ensure that I lead others to Christ. I am a very slow reader, but when I read, God reveals the meaning of the scripture and His will for my life as a pastor at Miracle Valley Church in Tuscaloosa, Alabama. I do not move until I am instructed by the spirit of God. I do not pray for people just because they make the request; it is only by God's guidance that I move. Proverbs 3:6 says, "In all thy ways acknowledge him, and he shall direct thy paths."

I stay in touch with God through fasting and praying to ensure that I have the knowledge and wisdom to lead His people in a manner that He approves of. I do not hold my wisdom captive for my congregation. I am a man of God for all people who need a spiritual leader. All people of this world are entitled to the prayers and leadership of the church. They are all members of the body of Christ. God wants people who are not educated in His will to know that they have the same God who works with people who are educated in His will. "By stretching forth thine hand to heal; and that signs and wonders may be done by the name of thy holy child Jesus" (Acts 4:30). Miracles come through obedience.

God sent His Son to die on the cross so that we could have life and to give us the opportunity to get back our God-given inheritance. Jesus died and shed His blood to give us back the authority that was our birthright. If He had not died on the cross, we would not have the opportunity to eternal life. Adam and Eve were born with this same power. They were born with innocence and lost it by disobeying God. Once they became sinners, they lost their innocence and were ashamed of their bodies, so they tried to cover themselves.

We have the same power that Jesus did. Only by faith can we do what Christ did; we must have faith in God to make this possible. "And Jesus said unto them, Because of your unbelief: for verily I say unto you, If ye have faith as a grain of mustard seed, ye shall say unto this mountain, Remove hence to yonder place; and it shall remove; and nothing shall be impossible unto you" (Matthew 17:20).

A lot of people today do not know that we are forgiven of our past, present, and future sins. We are trying to get God to do His work over, although He did it two thousand years ago. We just have to accept God's word by faith and through grace.

Chapter 2

The Beginning

I never knew my parents and was raised in a foster home until the age of five. My siblings and I were not properly cared for in the foster home where we lived, so the authorities closed the home; they sat us on the porch, and whoever wanted us could take us. Two sisters came who lived about a mile apart; one took me, and the other took my brother. I was raised by an old generation of people, without access to my generation of people, while my brother was raised by a young family and had a better life and better opportunities. My little sister was taken by a Caucasian family, and I never heard from or saw her again.

When I was a child, clothing and food were scarce for me. I had one pair of pants for church and some clothes to work in; that was back when people built their own houses. I felt hurt that I was not raised with my generation. I also wanted to know my birth mother and father but never got a chance to find them. I felt I was raised twenty-three years backward, not keeping up with my generation. I stayed to myself and never got into a fight or other trouble.

I worked in the fields starting at seven years of age and continued doing that until I became an adult. At that time, I started a life of my own. Once things improved with my foster parents, they shared my earnings with me. I started off making fifty cents a day, and the amount later increased to seventy-five cents and eventually a dollar per day. When I could make a dollar, it felt as if I had found a gold mine.

From a young age, I wanted to have my own property. I was not old enough to buy property, so I gave my parents the money to buy the first five acres of land for me. A little while later, five more acres became available in the same area, and I purchased them, making me the owner of ten acres of land at a young age. The deeds were in my foster parents' names until I was old enough to own property. I was in my early twenties when my parents passed, and I inherited another five acres.

I realized I needed to make more money to save up to start my own farm, so I took a job at a mobile home factory, starting out as a janitor and later being promoted to the mailroom. I also worked in a rock pit using sounding rods. I dug out rocks that were carried out in trucks and taken to an area to get crushed. For each truck that I filled, I received fifty cents. As land became available for purchase, I purchased it. Eventually, I owned thirty acres of land, in the same area. I had a barn built on the property that was one hundred by forty feet in size.

God instructed me on how to put the farm together and earn money. When I fenced in the farm, He instructed me to start at the corner, go all the way around, and fence it in. Then I cut off sections for pastures so when the cattle were in one section, I could farm another area. To start, I purchased a little calf that I had to bottle-feed, and eventually, with God's help, I became the owner of seventy-five head of cattle.

I listened to what God told me to do. I met a minister who traveled all over the United States preaching the Gospel of Jesus Christ, and I went with him to different places, such as New York. I would leave one revival and go directly to the next revival with my belongings in the car. He went to places where people were working miracles, and I watched them and listened to how they were operating, and then I searched the scriptures to see if it was the word of God. God told me that if I left the ministry of others, He would reveal Himself to me.

I stayed on the road until 1979. I went to work in Mississippi and started a revival in a house that filled very quickly and became too small for the members. I was blessed to purchase a church and made another minister the pastor of that church. God led me to move to Alabama. I listened to the voice of God and continue to do the same today.

No one wanted to associate with me because I was not an educated man. I would always let God teach me what to say to the congregation, and it would encourage the people. It takes me a long time to read the scriptures, but that doesn't matter to me. I would shut myself off from the world, get into sackcloth, and sleep on the floor to keep myself from getting too comfortable and falling asleep. I needed to make a connection with God for His people. There were times when I went to a motel to get away from everyone and stayed there a week, but I did not eat or sleep in the bed. I slept on the floor, sometimes on rugs. I wanted to make sure that I was available to hear God when He spoke to me.

One time, I heard footsteps, but no one was there. God told me that they were the footsteps of evil spirits trying to figure out what I was doing and to distract me from hearing from God. He taught me how to recognize evil spirits and how they work. I could not work with others because they did not understand how I made contact with God, interpreting the scriptures without being educated enough to read much. The Spirit taught me what to do and how miracles and prophecies worked in my presence. My own people, including my foster family, rejected me. My aunt asked me, "Where did you come from? We don't have anyone like you in our family."

Miracles happen, but only through the spirit of God. Once, when I went to a revival, the preacher said that God told him if anyone had a pipe for drugs and left the tent that night with it, that person would fall dead. That night, before the service was over, the large platform was covered with pipes people gave up. Some members of the congregation came to church for a little while and felt that they could work the same miracles, so they started a church of their own. It later failed. Matthew 22:14 says, "For many are called, but few are chosen."

Many times, God will speak to us, but we do not wait to hear His instructions. I have been in this ministry for many years and still travel this road alone, but many ministries have started at Miracle Valley under my instructions and guidance. For this, I give all the glory to God.

Chapter 3

The Calling

I was called to preach in 1977 in Florida. People there were not comfortable with my closeness to God and did not agree with the miracles and healing that God manifested through fasting and praying. God would reveal Himself to me and instruct me on how to lead His people. For several years I was associated with another minister, but then God told me to move to Tuscaloosa, Alabama. This would be my first time on my own. God anointed me with His spirit and sent me out to witness to His people. He told me to go in 1977, but I did not leave until 1979.

At that time, I had a great farm and my own idea of how I wanted to live life. I did not want to let go of the farm. I was married with children and had a great family, and I did not see an immediate need to leave when God called me in 1977. I decided that it would be okay to go later, and I spent two years doing nothing but farming. The year that I kept farming after God told me to move, the crops were flourishing. I was excited to see things going so well and expected it would be the best harvest ever. Later in the year, however, there was no rain, and the dryness took a great toll on the crops. Everything began to wither because of the lack of water. We decided to try to find jobs to help support the family until we could plant another crop. "For my thoughts are not your thoughts, neither are your ways my ways, saith the Lord" (Isaiah 55:8). It is not good to deal with God's wrath; it is not a pleasant thing to overcome.

It finally rained, and the fields started to blossom and flourish again. I was excited to see the change. I finished working the crops and waited for harvest time. One day, I decided to check the field to see how things were going, and to my surprise, bugs and worms had almost destroyed the crops. It was awful. I had never seen so many insects in one field. This was devastating to farmers in the area. That year, the harvest was very scarce and made it hard for area farmers to take care of their families. We did not give up and looked forward to the next year's harvest.

Soon, it was spring again, and time to prepare the soil for planting the fields. We anticipated a great harvest. Things looked great, and we felt very excited about what the new harvest would bring to families in the area. We anticipated that the insects would be plentiful, so we treated the crops for insects ahead of time and planned to irrigate the crops during the drought season. We did everything in our power to avoid what had happened the year before. We prepared for a big harvest and were very excited. Later in the summer, however, the insects returned in an even larger number, and the other farmers were convinced that I needed to go, thinking God must not have been satisfied with my delay in leaving.

My disobedience caused other farmers and families to suffer, just as Egypt suffered during the Exodus because of the pharaoh. "Then the Lord said unto Moses, Go in unto Pharaoh, and tell him," Thus saith the Lord God of the Hebrews, Let my people go, that they may serve me" (Exodus 9:1). Because of Pharaoh's disobedience, all of Egypt suffered ten plagues and, worst of all, the loss of their firstborn. It is important that we understand our lives are not our own to do what we will with, because our actions affect others around us.

When the insects destroyed the crops and farmers did not know how they would feed their families with no harvest, I realized that it was time for me to talk to God and see if He would hear my prayers even though I had disobeyed His instructions. I needed Him to work on my behalf for myself and other farmers. I told God if He blessed me with a good harvest that year, I would do His will for the rest of my life. I had no room to bargain with God, but knew that He was a merciful God and would forgive my disobedience as long as I asked sincerely.

Soon after that came the rain, and everything changed. God told me to go out to the field, and I said, "Why? There isn't anything out there." Just for obedience's sake, I went to the field and was amazed by how things had changed. The corn was so high it was above my head; leaves were long and drooping. Each stalk had three ears of corn on it. The corn was so plentiful I had to hire a combine to harvest it.

Trucks soon lined up one after another, with people waiting to buy watermelon. My watermelons were not irrigated. If the watermelons received too much water, they would not be sweet. I had paid to have the fields irrigated before the rain came, so the devil tried to distract me. The devil then said to me, "See there; see how you lost all that money?" The devil tried to distract me so I would not see God's blessings. "The thief cometh not, but for to steal, and to kill, and to destroy" (John 10:10). Satan will distract you by showing you all the negative things; even a small thing could block a huge blessing.

After that, I started selling everything. I took all my equipment and things I had purchased with the farm and gave them to other farmers. If I owed money on the equipment, I gave it back to the company from which I purchased it. I gave away all I did not sell, and I moved to Alabama.

Because of my obedience to God, miracles were performed. A woman with a brace on her leg who could barely walk had the desire to be healed. I prayed for her. I said to her, "You can't get married like this; you won't be any good to anybody or yourself." I asked her to raise her hands, and she did not hesitate to obey. God healed her that night. She was so excited about God's blessing she could not contain herself. We were at a local school where the revival was being held. She ran down the hallway to the gym, where the people were playing basketball. She was so excited and people were so amazed that she shut the game down. She was totally healed that night.

There was an incident where a lady was in jail and she was the talk of the town. Town conversation said that she would not get out of jail. The spirit of God told me that she would be out of jail by Friday. I waved the staff toward the courthouse as the spirit instructed me; the spirit told me to tell the people that she would be out of jail and at church on Friday, and she was. "And he said unto them, this kind can come forth by nothing, but by prayer and fasting" (Mark 9:29).

God still works miracles now if you allow Him to work in your life.

Chapter 4

You Must Cultivate the New Seed

Father, thank You for Your people. Thank You for the ones who are here. Thank You for the ones who are coming. Thank You for the ones who are not. Speak to them wherever they are; they are your children, and you have every right to speak to them in the name of Jesus. And we thank you for it in Jesus's name. Amen.

"Wisdom is the principal thing; therefore get wisdom: and with all thy getting get understanding" (Proverbs 4:7).

It is very important that we understand God's will for our lives; this is something that we often overlook. We must cultivate the new seed that God has planted in our hearts. A seed is no good until it's planted in the right soil. It cannot grow until it's planted; it has nowhere to grow. You cannot bring forth fruit unless you are planted in the right soil, where you can be rooted in God. If we cultivate God's will and word in our hearts, we will bring forth godly fruit.

Most trees you see will naturally bring forth fruit. You can always buy green grapes at the grocery store; some are sweet, some are sour, and some have no taste at all, but they are all green grapes. It is the same with the children of God. We are all His children, but most of the time, as children of God, we work with the flesh, and when you work with the flesh, you are not cultivating what God gave you.

God gives us new seeds, not old seeds. The point is that we need to know what the new seeds are. If you don't know what the new seeds are, God cannot plant them in you. You cannot do the will of God if you do not know His will for your life. There are times when God tries to move us in a new direction and we hold on to the old instructions. If you can't let go of the past, you will never move into the future. The new seeds are the revelation of God's will for your life.

The spirit of God reveals three new seeds: love, faith, and power. These have to be cultivated in the spirit and not in the flesh. Love in the natural will leave room for hate and unbelief, because there is no power to restrain the love and faith. The spirit of God is what gives you the power to cultivate love and faith. When you hear people talk about doing things and see no action, they haven't cultivated the new seed that lie dormant. We do not take the time to cultivate the seeds; the spirit of God. God gives us so many gifts, but we do not take the time to cultivate our gifts, and because we do not, we have no strength to overcome the power of Satan.

People will help you cultivate the negative and turn away from the positive. People love darkness because they think that it hides their evildoing. "And this is the condemnation, that light is come into the world, and men loved darkness rather than light, because their deeds were evil" (John 3:19). No matter what is done in the dark, good or evil, it will manifest itself in the light. The darkness will never overcome the light, evil will never win over good, and Satan will never outshine God. In every evil and bad disaster, God's light shines through; people pull together in a manner that destroys all the evil. All the focus is on how we overcome the disaster with the help of strangers, no matter their color, size, faith, or economic status. This is true, but evil does not want to accept it. I was lying in my bed when God told me to discuss this just as plainly as I am speaking to you.

The reason that bad things happen is because we cultivate the wrong seeds: the seeds of doubt, fear, and unbelief. If you cultivate them, those are what's working. I'm telling you that you are looking at a man who is tired of foolishness. Somebody asked me, "Well, why are you tired of foolishness?" I am tired of foolishness because of the God in me. We keep asking God to do things that He has already done. We say, "Lord, I want You to do this for me." Have you ever considered that it's already been done?

"Hear ye therefore the parable of the sower. When any one heareth the word of the kingdom, and understandeth it not, then cometh the wicked one, and catcheth away that which was sown in his heart. This is he which received seed by the way side. But he that received the seed into stony places, the same is he that heareth the word, and anon with joy receiveth it" (Matthew 13:18–20).

The average person right now is dealing with the words of the world, not the words of the kingdom. This means not understanding the following: "My people are destroyed for lack of knowledge: because thou hast rejected knowledge, I will also reject thee, that thou shalt be no priest to me: seeing thou hast forgotten the law of thy God, I will also forget thy children" (Hosea 4:6). We are not void of understanding; you may not follow it, but you are not void of His word. You know God said it and God will do it, but you just don't want to do it as He said to do it. We make the choice to do it the way we want to in order to benefit our needs, but there are no shortcuts when it comes to God's word and living the holy life that He has set for us to live. "I call heaven and earth to record this day against you, that I have set before you life and death, blessing and cursing: therefore choose life, that both thou and thy seed may live" (Deuteronomy 30:19).

We have a moral obligation to choose good, but not a legal obligation. God will not force you to do what is good and righteous; He is not the sheriff of your conscience. God gives us freedom to do what we will with our lives, but we will reap the results of our choices, good or bad. You cannot plant apple seeds and expect to reap oranges; you cannot plant sweet potatoes and reap white potatoes. You can only harvest what you planted. "Be not deceived; God is not mocked: for whatsoever a man soweth, that shall he also reap" (Galatians 6:7).

We sometimes wonder why so many things come against us and whether they have a right to. Satan isn't a spirit to play with; he has power also, and he is always trying to pull you away from God Spirit. Jesus said, "The thief cometh not, but for to steal, and to kill, and to destroy: I am come that they might have life, and that they might have it more abundantly" (John 10:10). My job as a servant of God is to help you understand the will of God for your life. If natural food is taken away from you, you will starve to death in about thirty to sixty days; every day, you'll get weaker and weaker. Your spirit will starve the same way if you do not feed it spiritually.

You may say to someone, "I'm thinking about buying a yacht." Then he or she may reply, "You know good and well you can't afford that." Satan plants this spirit of doubt in your mind through that person. This is how Satan comes to steal and destroy what is rightfully yours. "If ye then, being evil, know how to give good gifts unto your children, how much more shall your Father which is in heaven give good things to them who ask him?" (Matthew 7:11). The yacht is yours just for the asking. God already made this possible through love, faith, and power. If you are in agreement with the other person, you are stealing from yourself. God's already told you what's yours. All you've got to do is cultivate what He has given to you—the love, the faith, and the power. Cultivating that will get you everything you desire.

The lack of understanding gives Satan room in your mind. You should stand flat-footed right then and there and say, "Hold on just a minute. God said it." Your faith is what will shut the door on Satan. When you say, "God said it," it takes the power away from Satan. I hope that I can explain this so everyone can understand what I am trying to say. I'm tired of God's people not having the things that they desire and deserve. We should have life according to 3 John 1:2: "Beloved, I wish above all things that thou mayest prosper and be in health, even as thy soul prospereth." People hear me talking about yachts and all these kinds of things because they are ours for the asking.

Jesus said that He took poverty and gave us prosperity. He took poverty and died so we could have prosperity. It is sad when we say that we are the children of God and we have nothing to show for it. If you are a child of rich parents, you should have the same as your parents have because you were born to them. It is the same way with the children of God. We are His children, and all who ask are born into the family of wealth and good health.

You allow Satan to tell you that you do not deserve a family, a home, a companion, or whatever you desire. Satan tells you that you must be perfect. He brings all the wrong things that you have done into your mind. Satan knows that if he can control your mind, it's just a matter of time before your body will follow.

Matthew 5:45 says, "That ye may be the children of your Father which is in heaven: for He maketh his sun to rise on the evil and on the good, and sendeth rain on the just and on the unjust." God loves us all no matter what we do or say. He wants us to be good children, but He gives us a choice. Our lives will be more pleasing in God's sight if we live righteously. You will reap what you have sown, and He has no control over your choices about whether to be perfect to earn His blessings.

A thief like Satan can't steal from you unless you allow him to. In our natural lives, we prepare our homes to keep thieves out by installing security systems and weapons to defend ourselves just in case a thief successfully enters our domain. It is the same with God; He has put a magnetic spiritual field around you, and when a thief comes, the field alerts you that the enemy is on the prowl. You may not see anything, but you know something is out there because the alarm didn't go off for nothing. God does not set off false alarms. If one goes off, take heed and relax. Satan will not penetrate the hedge of protection that God has placed around you. Satan will not do it.

A lot of people are hooked on what God's going to do, but no, but He doesn't have to do anything. He has done it already. Job loved his wife. Job never told his wife she was like one of those foolish women. As Job loved his wife; he would have never degraded her because of her foolish words, he loved her too much. If he had called her foolish, he would have had a foolish woman, but he never said that. Job looked at it like this: *She was the mother of his children, and she has been with him all this time. I'm not going to call her foolish, because I love her. But she sounds like one.* Job 2:9 *Then said his wife unto him, Dost thou still retain thine integrity? Curse God and die.*

Consider this: "He also that received seed among the thorns is he that heareth the word; and the care of this world, and the deceitfulness of riches, choke the word ..." (Matthew 13:22).

Choke the word. All right, if somebody come up with something else other than what God said, that chokes it. Or when someone tries to deceive and distract you from the word of God, they are choking you, taking the life away from you. Naturally, so when someone chokes you, you are out of breath and soon there will be no life in you. This is the same with the spirit of God.

We are dealing with a simple gospel. It's not hard. Our gospel is the same way with the Spirit of God. The word of God is simple. It adds no sorrow. When we change, the world will change, but the world can't change until we change. The Spirit demonstrates love, faith, and power; the world doesn't have those. We are going to the wrong source for love, faith, and power, going to the world. It doesn't have them.

"... and he becometh unfruitful" (Mark 13:22).

You become the kind of fruit that the world look for but you can't produce it without the spirit of God, you are unfruitful. If He looks for sweet oranges and you don't have anything but bittersweets, that's not His fruit. You know what kind of fruit I'm talking about? You know, I say, she says, they say—the wrong fruit. "Well, I say, she says, they say." And nobody comes up with what Jesus said: the wrong fruit.

Consider this: "But he that received seed into the good ground is he that heareth the word, and understandeth it; which also beareth fruit …" (Matthew 13:23).

What kind of fruit are you bearing? Bitter or sweet?

"… and bringeth forth, some a hundredfold, some sixty, some thirty" (Matthew 13:23).

Some receive it, what, a hundredfold, some sixty, some thirty. Our goal is to produce a hundredfold by growing in the Spirit of God. We must not judge those who are not at one hundred, love and patience will get them there. As we sometimes judge people who come into the church not dressed as we think that they should be, act as we think that they should, they are not at a hundred fold. They are growing: some sixty, but they are growing. How long do I have to wait for thirties and sixties? He said the thirty will grow. That's why the ones with the hundred have to keep teaching.

Jesus had a hundredfold ministry, but he had to keep teaching until we receive the hundred. Accept that you are growing, and when you get to a hundred, help others grow. Come on, sixty; come on, thirty. They are growing, aren't they? Now, what will He have? He'll have a whole army of a hundredfold. God has planted his love in you and if you cultivate that, you will grow in love and in faith. The enemy can't do anything to you because you have the fullness of God.

We must perfect our ministry before we go out and try and reach others. We must know what we are teaching. For many are called but few are chosen. (Matthew 22:14). We move before we know what He wants us to do for him. This causes a lot of failed ministries. There are times when God wants us to be a missionary and we become a preacher because we did not want to see what God was saying to us. We do not wait until the seed take root in our heart. We must cultivate the seed that God has planted within our heart. Everyone was not called to be a leader, some just a follower. On every corner you will find a church with a few members. It's because we move on our own, not looking to the will of God, it's what we want to do and this brings about division among people.

Just because you have a good testimony you are not necessarily called to preach and lead people. There are times when we just do not want to be subject to others and follow leadership. We all must be accountable to someone. If you can't follow, you definitely can't lead. Leaders are made by cultivating the seed that is planted in their heart, giving it time to grow, take good root and is nourished by the Spirit of God, before we take out on a journey.

1 Corinthians 3:18. "Let no man deceive himself. If any man among you seemeth to be wise in this world, let him become a fool, that he may be wise." If you are patience you will receive: faith, love, and power. Satan doesn't like this and doesn't know how to deal with it. When you have those three things, you lack nothing. You've got His love. You've got His faith. You've got His power. When we move without faith, love and power, this makes you an easy target for Satan, because the seed has not been cultivated and grown to maturity. If you just be patient God will equip you with what you need to do his will and the job He has called you to do. Once your heart is in it, God will take care of the flesh. If you have faith you have what God says you can have. If you want a yacht, you do not have to settle for a paddle boat. A car, don't settle for a jalopy. We sometimes settle because of our lack of faith and the weak seed that has no root because we didn't give it time to grow before we plucked it up. Satan comes at us when we are weak in the Spirit of God.

Luke 8:5-8 "A sower went out to sow his seed: and as he sowed, some fell by the way side: and it was trodden down, and the fowls of the air devoured it. And some fell upon a rock; and as soon as it was sprung up, it withered away, because it lacked moisture. And some fell among thorns; and the thorns sprang up with it, and choked it. And other fell on good ground, and sprang up, and bare fruit an hundredfold. And when he had said these things, he cried, He that hath ears to hear, let him hear."

Some of the seed fell on stony ground. There was not enough soil for them to catch hold in the soil and as soon as the sun came out they withered because they had no depth. This is what happens to the uncultivated seed in our heart. Some fell in thorns, and some in good soil.

The person that takes off as soon as they think that God sent them, they soon give up because they have not power to withstand the power of Satan. Those that fell among the thorns, the evil people of the world. Their spirits of worldly were stronger than theirs and they were overcome by the world's influences.

Their faith was stronger than your faith in God. The seed was not cultivated. Some of the seed fell in good soil and took the time to grow and listen to the word of God from a fruitful soldier of God, prayed, worked with them and learned all that they needed to go out in the world to minister the word of God. They were strong and nourished with the Spirit of God, so they were able to bring others to Christ and not be overtaken by the evil spirits in the world. They were very fruitful because they took their time to be cultivated and grow in the Spirit of God. it. You will multiply one hundred fold, you will bring other souls to Christ. Not of our own power but by the power of God that his word has been cultivated in our hearts.

Chapter 5

Miracles on Elm Street

The church on Elm Street grew fast, people left other churches and came to Elm Street, where people were being delivered from long time headaches; one young girl was healed and was able to walk again after doctors told her mother that she would never walk again. The sprit told me to tell her mother that she would walk again. I prayed for the young lady, and she rejoiced for about fifteen minutes and she never used crutches again.

One young man was casting out demons and Satan confronted him, threatening to expose him if he didn't stop preaching the word of God and doing miracles. He prayed for people with no jobs, and they received them. One young lady was in debt, and she was about to lose her home. The next day, she received three checks, and she testified to the church of the miracle.

The church building had termites; they waited until I got on the floor to preach, and then they started flying all over the place. This was just another of Satan's tricks to distract people from God's message. We had no money to pay the bills or get rid of the termites, but I kept teaching the word of God. I did a lot of praying and seeking God. I would get rugs and sleep on them, but they were as hard as the floor. I went on praying for three to four days at a time to hear from God for the people. I would stay away for several days trying to hear from God, grow strong in His Spirit. I would not sleep in the bed because I didn't want to get too comfortable and lose my connection with God.

One night, a man came to my house and said, "Are you all having church tonight?" He was well dressed for church. When I said we were not having church, he replied, "But I heard you all having church and I came to join the church." He was an alcoholic, he attended later and God saved him. He later backslid, and I told him that God had saved him and he could not go back to the same crowd anymore. One Sunday, the man came to me in spirit at church, I stepped aside to let him in. The congregation saw me step aside, but they did not see the spirit of the man. Later I was told the man had died that day. His spirit walked through the church as he passed on to the spirit world.

The ministers worked for hard to cast demons out of a lady a church on night. Her face was away from the door. The member continues to try to cast out the demons. When I arrived and went into the church, the lady said, "Oh no!" Her husband knew that she had seen me walk in, the demons in her left in an instant.

Demons

Can a Christian have a demon? Christians cannot be possessed. A Christian cannot be possessed with demons, because the Spirit of God occupies the place in your heart.

"Neither give place to the devil" (Ephesians 4:27).

"How God anointed Jesus of Nazareth with the Holy Ghost and with power: who went about doing good, and healing all that were oppressed of the devil; for God was with him" (Acts 10:38).

"Submit yourselves therefore to God. Resist the devil, and he will flee from you" (James 4:7).

"And again, departing from the coasts of Tyre and Sidon, he came unto the sea of Galilee, through the midst of the coasts of Decapolis" (Mark 7:31).

"And they that had eaten were about four thousand: and he sent them away" (Mark 8:9).

Matthew 12:43 says "When the unclean spirit is gone out of a man, he walketh through dry places, seeking rest, and findeth none"

Galatians 5:20-21, "Idolatry, witchcraft, hatred, variance, emulations, wrath, strife, seditions, heresies, envyings, murders, drunkenness, revellings, and such like: of the which I tell you before, as I have also told you in time past, that they which do such things shall not inherit the kingdom of God" (Galatians 5:20–21).

Romans 8:13, "For if ye live after the flesh, ye shall die: but if ye through the Spirit do mortify the deeds of the body, ye shall live".

1 Peter 5:8, "Be sober, be vigilant; because your adversary the devil, as a roaring lion, walketh about, seeking whom he may devour".

"The thief cometh not, but for to steal, and to kill, and to destroy: I am come that they might have life, and that they might have it more abundantly".

Can a person be possessed by more than one demon? Yes, people can be possessed by many demons when you let one demon in then it can open the door for others. You must deal with demons using your spirit, demons only move by the word of God. Demons goal is possessing a Christian's heart. They always speak contrary to the word of God. This is Satan's way into your heart. The Spirit of God will not occupy the same place with evil.

"The men of Nineveh shall rise in judgment with this generation, and shall condemn it: because they repented at the preaching of Jonas; and, behold, a greater than Jonas is here. The queen of the south shall rise up in the judgment with this generation, and shall condemn it: for she came from the uttermost parts of the earth to hear the wisdom of Solomon; and, behold, a greater than Solomon is here. When the unclean spirit is gone out of a man, he walketh through dry places, seeking rest, and findeth none. Then he saith, I will return into my house from whence I came out; and when he is come, he findeth it empty, swept, and garnished." Then he goes and take with himself seven other spirits more wicked than himself, and they enter in and dwell there; and the last state of that man is worse than the first. So shall it also be unto this wicked generation."(Matthew 12:41–45).

We must make sure that we are filled with the Spirit of God before we tread on territory that we are not qualified to tread.

Chapter 6

Love as Christ Loveth

Matthew 18:20, "For where two or three are gathered together in my name, there am I in the midst of them."

You can have a small crowd, and God is still move as with the multitude of people. Where there is a multitude, there's trouble, there is more spirits to deal with. There are times when God's Spirit is stronger when there are few gathered together. There are fewer places for Satan to dwell. Evil spirits need places to dwell and that place is the heart of individuals. In most churches there are "clicks". There are group that thinks that they are better than everyone else because they make more than minimum wage. They feel that this gives them the right to look down on others. It's by the grace of God that we all make each day. Tall against short, fat against skinny, black against white, rich against poor and vice versa. No one can look down on others no matter what our status in life. Our priorities are in the wrong place. None of us can keep life in our own bodies no matter how rich, poor, tall, short, educated or what position we hold. God is the only spirit that can keep life in our bodies. So this puts all of us in the same ball park just trying to play the game. The only way we can get off that field and out of that ball park is to love as Christ loved. John 3:16 "For God so loved the world, that he gave his only begotten son, that whosoever believeth in him should not perish, but have everlasting life." How many of us can say that we are willing to sacrifice one of our children's life for people we do not know or people that we know or a family member?

We do not love as Christ loves. It is hard for us to love each other; family members, not outsiders, mother, fathers, sister and brothers. We hate each other for no reason, because of the evil spirit that dwells within us. One seed was not cultivated until maturity. It withered in the process.

We can go from place to place, one church to another, but if God is not in it, you aren't doing anything. There is a lot of showing off goes on in the church, pretending to know God, where is our truth? Our life tells other that we do not know God, you can tell by the life that you live, what you feel it in your heart, it comes out in action and your speech. "Death and life are in the power of the tongue" (Proverbs 18:21), not just talking, singing, praying, and shouting, "Hallelujah!"

That is not something you can do yourself, you are not qualified. The God in your heart wants to be released and free. We have a God who's bound up inside our heart and He wants to be free so He can use us to bring others to Christ.

1 Corinthians 13:2: "And though I have the gift of prophecy, and understand all mysteries, and all knowledge; and though I have all faith, so that I could remove mountains, and have not charity, I am nothing." This has been looked over so much, but Paul preached it. Notice what he said: "I." Paul didn't throw responsibility off onto anyone else; he brought it to himself. Our problem today is that we always point at somebody else. The key is whether you have faith so that it can go to someone else. Paul uses that from verse 1 to 13, talking about himself. It's not about what He's done; it's about what you can do. What God did, no man could do. He had to come Himself and do it. After Adam blew it, he couldn't trust anyone. God left the care of this world in the hands of men.

Paul said, "I have the gift of prophecy." A lot of people run around, saying they have faith, but Paul said, "I have all faith, so that I could remove mountains, and have not charity, I am nothing." Now, he didn't say, "I am not anything." He said, "I am nothing." In other words, he meant, "If you want to know the truth, I can't help anyone. If I don't have it myself, I can't put it out there." We can run around here and try to prove something to somebody, but if the proof doesn't come from God, we are just a sounding brass or a tinkling cymbal—no love. elf. A lot of self-righteousness goes on today, and self-righteousness doesn't help anybody. All it helps you do is stay in your mess.

1 Corinthians 12:8–10, 28. It doesn't matter what you have in your heart; if you don't have the word of God, then you are lost. God passes out gifts to those who can handle them, not just to those who are in church. He doesn't give a gift to you because of who you think you are. And whatever He gives, He gives it through love. If you are not in a position for love, He doesn't give it to you his gift.

This is about love, and God doesn't pass out anything unless He's doing it in love. Adam over looked God's love and blamed it on Eve. God made previsions for Adam and Eve and they never had any worries, just one request from God, Genesis 2:16-17 And the Lord God commanded the man, saying. Of every tree of the garden thou mayest freely eat: But of the tree of Knowledge of good and evil, thou shalt not eat of it: for in the day that thou eatest thereof thou shall surely die. God give all of us free will, and this was the same with Adam, he made the choice to disobey God. But God still loves us so much that he sent his son to redeem us and put us back in touch with the father. He was the only one who could put this world back in order as it should be. He could not come a spirit; He had to come in the flesh. He had to come just like a man and walk like a man. He talked like a man, but He didn't say what man said; He said what God said. He always said what His Father said, He did what His Father said, He set the world back in order. And it doesn't matter who tries to take it out of order; it's not going to come out.

If you don't have the word of knowledge by the same spirit but a different spirit, then the devil gave it.

It takes a foundation to create the rest of a building. Are you the foundation or the walls? If you are the foundation, then you allow the rest of the building to be built the way it should. You are the building's support. The building cannot stand without support. If a building was nothing but a foundation, when it rained, you would get wet. Your construction has to be in order because you have a foundation. The foundation makes sure that the building stands up. If you don't have the right foundation, when the foundation cracks, the building will separate. That's why Paul said he laid the foundation and he laid one no other man could lay. In other words, no other man could lay what he laid because the Chief gave him the power to lay it. He gave him the power to build it, and no other man could build the foundation as it was built. He had all that came from the Maker, and he built it just as He said. When this foundation is laid, no man can add to it; no other man can take from it.

God told Adam and Eve in the garden that if they ate of the tree of knowledge, they would surely die?" Well, didn't the enemy come along and tell them that they would not surely die? Satan, the enemy, came right along and changed it. He was listening and heard what God told them. Adam said, "I know that if I stay with what God said, I will live, but the enemy told him go ahead and disobey God, you will not die. Adam Disobeyed God and this put him out of the protection of God, Adam was put out of the garden. Genesis 3:23-24 Therefore the Lord God sent him forth from the garden of Eden, to till the ground from whence he was taken.

So he drove out man; ...

Some people say that He put the woman out; that's a lie. He put the man out, and she followed. It does not matter how many women are in this ministry; God is looking at the man. Why? He didn't say anything to the woman. He went to the man and said, "I told you what to do.

This building that God want us to build is on a sure foundation. Although he told Adam what to do in the garden of Eden, it takes all to build the building that God want to be built. He gives some the ability to be a plumber to run the waterline, some to run the electricity. Now, just because this man is an electrician doesn't mean that he's a plumber. When we get someone to work on our house, we get someone who says he's a plumber, but he will mess you up if he isn't a real plumber. People's problem is that they try to work in a profession that they are not qualified to do. They want to control your life, I don't have any business coming into your house, controlling your wife. This is the cause of many problems in families today, outsiders trying to do the job of a family member when they are not a member.

If they would have cultivated the love of God in their hearts, they will be directed by the spirit of God to keep out. People who want to make their own interpretation make room for Satan to come in the home and church.

Satan has to get in there where he can fool somebody to give him a ride. If the gifts of God manifest themselves in the church Satan will not stay around but for a short time. You do not try to put Satan out of the Church, the spirit of God will change him

23

or they will leave on their own. You don't put the devil out. No matter how you see that person, if they are a liar, they don't lie to man; they lie to the Holy Ghost, and they either end up physically dead or spiritually dead. Peter told Ananias, "You didn't lie to men; you lied to the Holy Ghost." And when Peter said that, Ananias fell dead. His wife came along three hours later and told the same lie, and she fell dead. You think that you can lie now and get away with it; the same Holy Ghost that killed in those days is still present today. We sometimes walk around thinking that we are alive, but we are dead people walking. You are spiritually dead. You aren't any good to yourself or anyone else.

Chapter 7

Love, True Love

In Luke 15:11-32, the love that the father had for the prodigal son was true love. He saw his son coming afar off; he did not wait until his son made it into the gate, he started running to meet him and welcome him back home as if he never left. One father gave him the best robe, the first ring and the largest feast he could put together. He did not throw in his face how and why he left home, he just welcomed him back into the family. God' love is the same, he does not bring up your sins, he doesn't dwell on your past, He is excited to have his son back home. God loves us so until he forget and forgive us in an instant.

We go into the world and do all the wrong that we desire and can figure out to do. When we are ready to leave the world and return home to Christ he forgives us faster than we can forgive ourselves. Love as Christ love.

When Jesus asked Peter if he loved Him and Peter answered yes, He asked three times. After the third time, Peter said, "You know that I love you then you know all things." God's love has always been looked over because we love with the flesh and it doesn't work. Many families have been destroyed because of fleshly love.

God loves us so that He gave His only begotten son. Man had no life at that point. Love is not what we can do for God but what God can do for us. If true love is in you, it will transfer through to your children. We love because someone loves us. God gave us love, and we were not thinking about it, but He loved us anyway. This generation is lost now because true love is missing. Not everyone knows how to love. People think that love is what you see, but love is what you feel. It's in the heart. They get love and lust confused because they love what they see and not with the heart. The word love is over used because of the eyes. We do not love with the heart. It is very powerful, and it fails not. Christ loves us for no reason.

I've seen people with mates who are still lonely. Even when they sit right beside you, you feel lonely, empty, and alone. It is very miserable to be in a relationship and still feel empty and lonely. There is still a void. What do people do in real love? One with love does and one without does nothing. Lightning and thunder do not mix. When people meet, they hit it off, and there is lightning, because you think that this is real love. You are excited and full of joy, but soon that feeling goes away. You thought that it was love but it was just lust and you are left with that unsullied feeling and the shock of the lighting are no longer felt. This is where the thunder comes in, working to get a feeling that never existed. Now there is a clash between the two that bring on thunder. There was never any true love to hold the relationship together.

When a man wanted to marry a woman had to work for that woman; he had to pay for that woman's hand in marriage. Man had nothing until God made Eve. Eve was part of Adam. He loved her because he was a part of her. Woman came out of man's side, and she belongs by his side, not in front of or behind him. If you are not keeping as a husband, she is available to any man because she has no keeper. You can't fault her if she finds someone else to fill the void.

A ring symbolizes togetherness in God's love. When you take that ring off your hand and do not wear it, it tells the world that you are available. Your boy sees you saying that she is available; do not get upset if the boy hollers at her. If you have that bone of true love, you will never take that ring off. The ring is a continuous circle, and it symbolizes God of true love. We do not realize the power of marriage vows; we say them just to complete the marriage ceremony.

When you get the body of a woman and not the heart, you have nothing. You cannot hold a woman with you just by having the body. If you love God with all your heart and do not love your mate, it is a lie. You cannot love and hate in the same breath. This is just like God and Satan living in the same house. It will not happen. In a counseling session, I asked a man if he loved his wife, and he said yes, but I have a spare, I asked him, "Aren't you supposed to take the spare everywhere you go just in case you need it?" He said yes. I said, "Take it home, and see how long it takes before its flat." We do things and make decisions not considering how other in our lives will fell and how it will affect their lives.

Most people try to make other people pay for things that they did not do. They live in the past, and it blocks their future. Their first relationship did not work because off your spare and you want the future husband or wife to pay for your mistakes. The past will never fit into the future there is no life there. How can I live off thirty-five cents a day in 2017, when in the past, it was very valuable? You could get a gallon of gas for thirty-two cents high premium, eighteen cents for regular. Henry Ford created the Ford Model T that you could walk beside the car and talk to the person driving. The only difference is riding versus walking. Will this fit in 2017? This is why you can't take the past of a relationship into the future relationship.

It is just like bonding two rods of iron together, and the bond does not break. It will break in other places but not in the place where it was bonded. We are not bonded together by love; love is the bond. A man can't hurt his wife without hurting himself, she is a part of himself. He carries the woman in his heart. The heart is the real you, it causes the body to function. Your body is the temple of the Holy Ghost. Your body belongs to God.

Jesus did not make people come out of their sins, He loved them out of their sins. Abraham and Sarah were old, and God renewed the body so Sarah and Abraham had a child because love changed their body, but the body will not change love.

"Behold, I am the Lord, the God of all flesh: is there anything too hard for me?" (Jeremiah 32:27).

Chapter 8

Your Mind Clothed in Christ's Peace

I know that people get tired of me telling them that you are already what you are, but somehow, you seem to think that I am not telling the truth. There is no way that Jesus Christ came here and half-did anything. Jesus died on the cross to redeem man back to God because he loved us. He was nailed to the cross, and there wasn't a hammer that could pull out the nails; it was there for keeps. He suffered for us and demonstrated real love that he had for us.

He did it all. Anything that happens through me now happens because Christ is in me. The men in the Bible cast out devils, but it was because Christ was in them, not because of something that they accumulated. Man is destroying by trying to be himself somebody he's not.

"He that commiteth sin is of the devil; for the devil sinneth from the beginning. For this purpose the Son of God was manifested, that he might destroy the works of the devil" (1 John 3:8).

. Your mind has to be clothed with Christ's peace. We are in spiritual warfare. We are not warring against flesh. We do that, but God told you not to give any place to the devil. So if you give the devil a place, you fight flesh. God is a spirit and Satan is a spirit, and that's spiritual warfare, flesh doesn't have anything to do with it.

When you have the peace of Christ, you are ready to face the enemy and attack them in everything they do. You can attack me and win, but you are not the winner; the winner is on the inside, in the heart of man. We are talking spiritual warfare. Every one of us right now is in spiritual warfare, not war of the flesh. If you don't stop fighting in the flesh your reward will be hell. The only time that Satan can do anything to you is when you don't have the peace of God., your mind has to be clothed in His peace, and when your mind is clothed in His peace, there is no battle you will go up against and not win.

Acts 21:13: "Then Paul answered, "What mean ye to weep and to break mine heart? for I am ready not to be bound only, but also to die at Jerusalem for the name of the Lord Jesus." You give a place to the devil when you back up, trying to do something that's already been done. Christ's peace won the battle. Christ had peace on the cross. He didn't cry, moan, or groan, He did that for us? In the ministry, we get in too big of a hurry and say things that God didn't say, and that makes them lies because God didn't say them.

In Acts 21:13, Paul was bound, but he had God's peace. He was not only ready to be bound, which he was, but also ready to die. If you die for Jesus, you die to live. If you put a seed in the ground before it can live, it dies. If that seed doesn't die, nothing comes out of it. When it dies, it pulls the outside shell off and leaves it, because it isn't any good, but the inside comes up and lives. What Paul says here is that he's not worried about suffering; he's ready to die. We scuffle so hard trying to live. Christ died, but didn't He say to arm yourself likewise? So if you don't die, the outside shell won't fall off so that the inside can rise.

Spiritual warfare does not have you cutting the fool; your flesh does. In spiritual warfare, you are on one side or the other. The only way you will be able to die is in God's peace. God's peace causes you to die because it takes you out of your flesh. First comes the stalk, then the blade, then the fruit, then the harvest; that's the inner man.

2 Timothy 4:6: "For I am now ready to be offered, and the time of my departure is at hand."

People blame God for things that he did not do. He does not break things, he puts them together. (2 Timothy 4:6).

You must have His peace. He defeated Satan with His peace.

2 Corinthians 5:8: "We are confident, I say, and willing rather to be absent from the body …" "… and to be present with the Lord."

2 Timothy 4:8: "Henceforth there is laid up for me a crown of righteousness …" God's peace, a crown of righteousness is laid up for you. He doesn't have to get it; it's laid up for him. Haven't you had something in your house that you didn't want others to get so you hid it away but it was laid up for you? You didn't have to work or strain for it; it was laid up.

If He said to love, then love. He will back up your love, and whoever hates you will be backed up too because whatever a man sows, he will reap.

Romans 1:16: "For I am not ashamed of the gospel of Christ …"

Paul didn't say all of us aren't ashamed. He knew he had Christ's peace. Those men who had Christ's peace didn't let anybody change them. They died with the peace of God. That's why they could face death the way that they did—because they had His peace. They had the mind-set that whatever happened to them, so be it.

"… for it is the power of God unto salvation to everyone that believeth …"

"… to the Jew first, and also to the Greek."

With the peace of God, you will be ready for anything that you face. When death faces you, you'll be ready. If persecution faces you, you'll be ready. The peace of God makes you ready. If you are warring against something, you don't have the peace of God; you are scared. Fear is of the devil. You don't have God's peace when you have fear. God's love removes all fear and doubt from our mind, God's loves conquers all.

Chapter 9

Trying to Serve God in the Wrong Format

We must be spiritually prepared for defensive warfare. You cannot fight this war without being full of the Holy Ghost. "And when they had prayed, the place was shaken where they were assembled together; and they were all filled with the Holy Ghost, and they spake the word of God with boldness" (Acts 4:31).

"He that committeth sin is of the devil; for the devil sinneth from the beginning. For this purpose the Son of God was manifested, that he might destroy the works of the devil" (1 John 3:8).

Anytime you don't do what the word of God says, you are sinning. Be careful how you do the will of God. "Verily, verily …" (John 14:12).

God is getting ready to work miracles, and you must be spirit filled to receive them. "Now when all the people were baptized, it came to pass, that Jesus also being baptized, and praying, the heaven was opened" (Luke 3:21).

Jesus saith unto them, My meat is to do the will of him that sent me, and to finish his work" (John 4:34).

God gave us power over the enemy. You cannot lead the church without the power of God. Satan does not fight fair; he will wait until you have used all your ammo, and then he'll come out with an automatic rifle and mow everything down, including the congregation. Luke 10:19 Behold, I gave you power to tread on serpents and scorpions, and over all the power of the enemy: and nothing shall by any means hurt you.

This is my purpose: to do the will of God, not man's will. This should be our goal. We perish because of a lack of understanding. We do not take the time to get an understanding from God; we just move forward in our own will, not waiting to get directions from God. You have no power to protect yourself or your people; God doesn't work that way. He equips whom He sends to do the work.

About the Author

I am Pastor Samuel Richardson Sr., born May 9, 1927, in Ocala, Florida. I had one brother, Elijah Richardson, and a sister, Rosetta Richardson, and we were left on the front porch of a closed foster-care facility when I was five. God brought me through the valley with no education. God still holds my hand and teaches me, Samuel Richardson Sr., at the age of ninety, how to teach others the will of God.

I am just a meager servant of God who is not worthy of the gift that God has given me. I am not an educated man, and I never knew my parents; sometimes, I feel all alone in this world. I sometimes wonder why I was given the gift of prophecy and healing when I sometimes feel unequipped to minister His precious gift. I feel that if I were more educated, people would accept what I have to say.

About the Book

I wrote this book with the hope that it encourages others to press forward and do God's will no matter how inadequate they might feel. "I have planted, Apollos watered; but God gave the increase" (1 Corinthians 3:6).

There have been times when I did not tell people what God told me to tell them because I felt inadequate and could not approach those people due to their status. Later, I realized that I could have saved them from pain and hurt if I had been confident enough to approach them. I know this is a way that Satan tries to push me off track, but through fasting and praying, I press on. I've realized that God gives His gifts to whomever He desires, and it requires no special skills to receive His precious mercy, love, and gifts.

Printed in the United States
By Bookmasters